Stop Wishing. Stop Whining. Start Leading Study Guide

Stop Wishing. Stop Whining. Start Leading Study Guide

Cynthia Kay & Doreen Bolhuis

Copyright © 2016 Cynthia Kay & Doreen Bolhuis
All rights reserved.

ISBN: 1537322370
ISBN 13: 9781537322377
Library of Congress Control Number: 2016914414
CreateSpace Independent Publishing Platform
North Charleston, South Carolina

Table of Contents

Introduction vii

Part 1: So, You Want to Lead................ 1
Chapter 1   Give Up the Fairy Tale: It's Up to You 3
Chapter 2   Unseen Barriers: Are You Getting in
            Your Own Way? 7
Chapter 3   Three Levels of Leadership 11
Chapter 4   Administrative Assistant, Manager, or Executive:
            It Is a Choice 15
Chapter 5   The Mind-Set: The Higher You Go, the More
            You Give 19
Chapter 6   You Can Have It All...Just Not All
            at the Same Time 23

Part 2: Do You Have What It Takes? 27
Chapter 7   Eleven Traits of True Leaders 29
Chapter 8   The Art of Balancing Leadership Traits 33
Chapter 9   Do You Have to Wait in Line? 37
Chapter 10   How to Be Leader Men Follow 41
Chapter 11   How to Be a Leader Women Follow 45

Part 3: What Not to Do 47
Chapter 12   Getting Emotional. 49
Chapter 13   Overthinking Your Decisions 53
Chapter 14   Using Upspeak and Other Annoying Habits. 57
Chapter 15   The Gender Game. 61

Part 4: What to Do 65
Chapter 16   Be a Strategic Thinker. 67
Chapter 17   Communicate with Power. 71
Chapter 18   Change What You Can Change 75
Chapter 19   Quit Being Boring: Lead with Style 79
Chapter 20   Consider a Leadership Coach 83
Chapter 21   Know When to Change Course and Evolve. 87

Introduction

For those who wish to become great leaders, the journey is lifelong. You will never truly "arrive" and will always learn new leadership lessons.

The *Stop Wishing. Stop Whining. Start Leading. Study Guide* is designed to stimulate thoughtful conversations to help every leader gain new insights. We believe there are takeaways in this book for all leaders regardless of gender or experience. Whatever your title or career goals, you will find one or more concepts to challenge you. We suggest you choose just a few areas you'd like to work on now and develop action steps to implement these changes.

There are three categories of questions included in the study guide:

- Personal Reflection questions are for your individual study. These provide an opportunity for you to analyze your personal situation, goals, aspirations, challenges, and barriers. In your personal study time, you can reflect on how the book topics apply to you individually and what the most important steps are for you now. You can become aware of barriers that stand in your way and create action steps to break through them.
- Group Discussion questions will enrich learning by posing questions to stimulate a broad discussion. These questions provoke thinking about how to apply the concepts in the

INTRODUCTION

book and will encourage group members to add additional thoughts from personal experience. Group members can share real-life examples and develop real-life solutions to leadership challenges. The diversity of perspectives will enhance learning for all leaders in the group.

- Questions for Men are written to invite men to the conversation. We want to promote inclusive conversations rather than exclusive ones. We think everyone can learn when men contribute their perspectives, experiences, and suggestions. We think that men will learn as they listen to the perspectives and experiences of women and women will learn from men in the group. We know that both genders have unique perspectives to enrich the discussion and add to their collective learning. And we know that when the best talent of each gender is combined effectively in the workplace, it empowers a company and its people to achieve the best results.

This book contains information that will challenge you throughout your leadership journey. That journey is never ending. Revisit the book in six months, one year, and other intervals in the future. We think that new concepts will strike you at different junctures in your career journey. The popular quote "When the student is ready, the teacher will appear" is true. This book can continue to be one of your teachers if you periodically review the material to look for the next leadership challenge.

Set the book aside temporarily as you work on the most important leadership principles now. Come back to the book throughout your leadership journey when you want to refresh your mind and discover new skills and concepts to work on. We are confident that there will always be something to challenge you. We sincerely hope that the *Stop Wishing. Stop Whining. Start Leading. Study Guide* will empower you with information and strategies to help achieve your career goals, for now and for the future!

Part 1: So, You Want to Lead

CHAPTER 1

Give Up the Fairy Tale: It's Up to You

Personal Reflection

1. How might the fairy-tale myth of "being saved" be subtly at work in your own psyche? Could this myth cause you to be passive when you should advocate for yourself? Are you waiting for someone to notice your good work and advocate for you? What action steps can you take to become your own advocate?

2. Think about your early years. Did parents, siblings, and influencers empower you to do and be your best? How? If not, what steps can you take to develop the courage, perseverance, and confidence to reach your true potential, to become active rather than reactive or passive?

GIVE UP THE FAIRY TALE: IT'S UP TO YOU

Group Discussion

1. Describe how you have seen the fairy-tale myth subtly at work in women you know. What effect can this have on career development? How does it affect leadership potential, promotions, bonuses, assignments?

2. How can you challenge and empower other women in your personal and professional life? What messages do women need to hear? How can you help provide the support for women to succeed on your teams, in your company?

3. What support systems might women create to enhance professional success and reduce stress? What are the dangers and symptoms when women neglect to implement support systems? What support systems do men commonly implement, and what can women learn from this?

Questions for Men

1. What do you think of the fairy-tale myth? How have you seen this at work in families and in the workplace?

2. How can you support, encourage, and challenge females to develop the courage and perseverance they need to succeed? What message does it send when women are given a "pass" rather than a challenge? What is the long-term result?

3. How can you challenge all coworkers and direct reports to reach their true potential? Are there situations in which you have given female professionals a pass rather than challenging them to grow? Describe a situation and how you can respond to it differently in the future.

CHAPTER 2

Unseen Barriers: Are You Getting in Your Own Way?

Personal Reflection

1. What would a big dream look like for your future? Why is this dream important to you? What inner feelings does this dream invoke? How could you develop a strategy for manageable steps toward this dream?

2. Be honest with yourself and assess whether your focus at work has sometimes been internal (on yourself and your feelings) or external (on the company and results). How will you increase your focus on problem solving and results? How will you guard against blaming or complaining? Is there a friend, family member, or colleague who can support you and challenge you in this realm? If so, how will you develop a system to check your leadership attitude when facing workplace challenges?

Group Discussion

1. In what situations can you step forward instead of back? What projects, assignments, committees, teams, organizations, and so on can you engage in to utilize your expertise and develop your leadership skills? How can you become more assertive rather than passive in your career development?

2. In what situations might you have experienced gender bias? How can you move forward toward your goals in these situations? Share strategies that you have used in the past or can use in the future. How can you tactfully and carefully go around an obstacle if you can't go through it?

Questions for Men

1. How can you encourage female colleagues or direct reports toward more active engagement in meetings, projects, and problem solving? How can you facilitate opportunities for these women to face fears and develop greater courage and confidence?

2. What are situations in which you have witnessed gender bias? How can you lead in these situations to focus forward and create opportunities for women and men to succeed?

CHAPTER 3

Three Levels of Leadership

Personal Reflection

1. Considering the foundational concepts of level-one leadership, which ones currently provide a strong foundation for you now? What are the qualities you will need to master for the future? What action steps and strategies can you follow to strengthen your leadership foundation in these areas?

2. What is your current leadership level? Considering your values and preferences, what do you think is the best leadership level for you right now? For the future? Why?

Group Discussion

1. Share your experiences with "bosses" versus "leaders." What are the qualities and characteristics you have observed in each? How do these characteristics contribute to or detract from productivity and motivation for team members and the success of the company?

2. Discuss the costs and benefits, risks, and rewards of each leadership level. What are the most common levels of leadership for women? What factors contribute to this? Share your personal leadership preference and the reasons for this choice. How and why might the choice of leadership level change in different life stages?

Questions for Men

1. What are your experiences, both positive and negative, with "bosses" and "leaders"? Share your thoughts regarding the value of each style and your strategies to work with each. Do you think one is more effective than another? If so, which is more effective and why?

2. What is your current level of leadership? What risks and rewards have you experienced on your leadership journey? What insights can you share about the three levels of leadership and finding the best level at each stage of life?

CHAPTER 4

Administrative Assistant, Manager, or Executive: It Is a Choice

Personal Reflection

1. List your top gifts and talents and compare them with some of the examples in this chapter. What job realms might best utilize your natural gifts? Does your current position provide the daily reward of using your gifts? If not, what steps can you take toward a more fulfilling position?

2. Describe your ideal personal and professional life. What would your daily work be like? Your schedule? Your company? Your coworkers? Your residence, location, and personal lifestyle? What job realms might be best to achieve these ideals now and in five, ten, and fifteen years?

Group Discussion

1. Discuss the idea of thoughtfully planning your career and lifestyle versus yielding to the expectations of others or simply taking whatever opportunity presents itself. What primary and secondary factors should you consider in career planning? What are the challenges, and how can you stay focused on your goals during your career development? How can you balance focus with opportunity and life changes?

2. Discuss your own successes and setbacks in finding the right job realm. What has helped you? What hindered you? Share insights from your journey of discovery.

Questions for Men

1. Consider family members and coworkers who have navigated their professional journey skillfully and those who have not. What are the factors that contributed to greater success? Think also about your own career journey, and share insights from various job titles you have held.

2. How can you help inspire and encourage female professionals or family members toward jobs that utilize their natural gifts and talents? How important is this fit and why? What are some consequences of taking a job that is not the best fit for your gifts and talents? How can professionals be intentional about their career planning?

CHAPTER 5

The Mind-Set: The Higher You Go, the More You Give

Personal Reflection

1. What insights about your own mind-set did you gain from the "Analyze Your Inclination" exercise? How will these guide and inform your leadership journey?

2. Noting the unique strengths of women, how might these strengths also become a weakness for you? What action steps can you take to be more assertive in using your female strengths? What should you be cautious of, and how will you do this?

Group Discussion

1. Discuss the unique strengths of female leaders as discussed in this chapter. How have you observed these as both strengths and weaknesses in female leaders? How can you improve your own risk taking, decision making, focus, accountability, or other attributes presented in this chapter? How can you challenge coworkers and direct reports to grow in these areas?

2. Sound and timely decision making is a requirement in leadership. What guiding principles do you use in making leadership decisions? What holds you back? How can you improve in making assertive and timely decisions? How do you discern when to courageously forge ahead and when to be more cautious?

Questions for Men

1. Describe a situation when you have noticed excessive socializing in the workplace among women. What was the effect on coworkers and productivity? How did this affect your opinion of these professionals? What guidelines can female professionals and leaders follow in this realm?

2. Consider the strengths of the female brain as presented in this chapter. How can you help leverage these strengths for your company, department, and team? How might these opportunities be missed? What gets in the way? What can companies do to leverage female leadership strengths?

CHAPTER 6

You Can Have It All...Just Not All at the Same Time

Personal Reflection

1. What gets you excited about the future? What are your most important career goals? Why are these goals important to you? What is your time frame for achieving these goals? Write your goals and timelines, and review these periodically as you develop your career.

2. What are your priorities for the next twelve months? What are your next steps? What are some things you need to let go of to move forward and accomplish your goals? What could sabotage your success? How will you clear these barriers? When do you plan to start?

Group Discussion

1. Discuss career mapping. What might success look like at each stage of life and over a lifetime? How have you planned for and managed your own career development? What resources were helpful to you?

2. How do you think women can maintain work-life balance and still achieve career goals? What does success in this realm look like to you? What have you tried so far, and how has that worked? What things do you need to stop doing? What do you need to start doing?

Questions for Men

1. What support systems help you and other male professionals achieve your career goals? Evaluate your own work-life balance. What have you learned, and what can you share about this? What challenges have you faced? How have you managed these challenges?

2. Share your thoughts on career mapping. How do end-game goals influence actions and choices? What have you learned from your personal experience or from colleagues and mentors? How and why have you adjusted your career goals over time?

Part 2: Do You Have What It Takes?

CHAPTER 7

Eleven Traits of True Leaders

Personal Reflection

1. Read and reflect on the description of "passionate." What are you passionate about and why? How does this inform your leadership journey and ultimate career goals?

2. Which of the leadership traits are the strongest for you? Which traits need work? Identify one trait you'd like to improve. What is the most important action you can take to improve this trait? When will you start? What changes do you think this will create? What will the results look like?

Group Discussion

1. Discuss the effects of leadership traits on an organization, team, family, nation, etc. How do true leaders exhibit and utilize these traits?

2. Consider the effect of "boss" type people who possess a title but have not developed their leadership traits. What is the impact on the organization and its people? How can you develop your own leadership style, and what does this look like for you?

3. Are there traits that you consider essential and traits that might be secondary? Why? What traits do you think are essential at all leadership levels? What traits are particularly essential for Level Three leaders? Why?

Questions for Men

1. Which traits do you particularly admire in a leader? Why? Do you think men place a higher value on some of these traits than women? If so, which ones and why?

2. What traits do you think are essential for female leaders who aspire to executive positions? Why? What are some pitfalls of female leaders you've observed, and which of these traits would improve their leadership success?

CHAPTER 8

The Art of Balancing Leadership Traits

Personal Reflection

1. Review your strong and weak leadership traits from chapter 7. How will development of your weak traits improve your leadership balance? What changes do you think this will create in your leadership impact?

2. What would success look like for you in leadership balance? What steps can you take to improve your balance? Specifically, how will you measure your progress?

THE ART OF BALANCING LEADERSHIP TRAITS

Group Discussion

1. Consider your company's current challenges, goals, and projects. What leadership traits do you think should be utilized most prominently now? Why? Give examples of how these traits might be used to move the company forward.

2. What have you learned about leadership balance from your "failures" or frustrations? How have you developed stronger traits as a result of past experiences? Share how you strengthened your leadership traits and how they have impacted your leadership?

Questions for Men

1. Is there a pattern of common strengths and weaknesses in leaders you have worked with? If so, share these with the group. What traits could be strengthened in leaders you know, and how would this create greater balance? How would this balance produce better results?

2. Which of the traits do you believe are essential for Level Three executives? Why? Which are less important? Why? What traits are essential for Level Two managers? Why? Finally, what traits are most important for Level One leaders? How does the development and use of balanced leadership traits affect career goals?

CHAPTER 9

Do You Have to Wait in Line?

Personal Reflection

1. What are your personal career aspirations and goals for now and for the future? What are you afraid of as you think about achieving these goals? Is there a potential path forward in your current company? Have you been an active advocate or a passive one for your career advancement? What actions can you take to step out of line and move forward? Write some goals and timelines for your next steps.

2. When was your most recent resume update? What new education, certifications, or other achievements have you added in the past year? What does your current reading list look like, and does it consistently include materials that challenge and inform you professionally? Update your resume if necessary, to be prepared for any future opportunity. Upgrade your reading list if necessary.

Group Discussion

1. Discuss the dynamic and observable traits of professionals who step out of line and get ahead. What sets them apart? How have they been active, versus passive, to achieve their career goals? What are some actions you and others can take now to "step out of line"?

2. How have you updated your resume in the past year? If you haven't, why? Discuss opportunities in your company, industry, community, etc. for you to grow professionally. How can these position you for future career opportunities? How can these make you more successful in your current position? What action will you take in the next year to grow professionally and update your skills and resume?

Questions for Men

1. Share your own strategies for career advancement. How have you prepared yourself for future opportunities? If you are in a management or executive position, what do you expect from direct reports who wish to advance? What successful strategies have others used that you can share?

2. How important is regular communication with supervisors regarding your goals and aspirations? What effect could this have on career opportunities? What are appropriate ways to communicate? What are harmful ways to communicate? What are ways to communicate outside of yearly evaluations? How does daily behavior and performance support or undermine your stated goals?

CHAPTER 10

How to Be Leader Men Follow

Personal Reflection

1. Reflect on your own leadership style, professional conduct and character. Are you currently achieving the leadership results you desire? If not, how will you grow in your leadership and what behavior(s) do you need to change first? What are action steps to improve your leadership?

2. What do you need to stop doing to be more respected as a female leader? What do you need to start doing?

Group Discussion

1. Have you worked with female leaders who were queen bees, office moms, alpha females, or supporters of an old girls' club? What was your experience and reaction to these women? Share any experiences with female "boss" types and their effect on the workplace. What are some steps to improve?

2. Discuss the descriptions of authenticity, company woman, industry expertise, self-discipline, and clear communication. How do these qualities generate respect? Do you believe some are more important for women than others? If so, why?

Questions for Men

1. What are the qualities that gain your respect for women leaders? In contrast, what attitudes and behaviors cause you to doubt or resist a woman's leadership? What suggestions can you offer?

2. What do you wish women leaders would do more of? What do you wish female leaders would do less of? Describe how these changes would produce better results in the workplace.

CHAPTER 11

How to Be a Leader Women Follow

Personal Reflection

1. How do you respond if a woman resists your leadership? How can you change your behavior to gain more respect as a leader? How can you use questions effectively for greater understanding? (A great resource is *Power Questions* by Andrew Sobel and Jerold Panas.)

2. Are you consistently even tempered in the workplace? Do you rise above pettiness to stay focused on problem solving and action steps? Are you equitable and free from bias among colleagues and direct reports? Honestly evaluate your inner attitudes, and strive to shift toward the leadership qualities you need to develop.

Questions for Men

1. What have you observed about female interaction in the workplace when there is conflict or resistance? What were the core issues you observed? Describe the behavior. What effect did this have on you and others in the workplace? What was effective or ineffective? What advice can you offer to female leaders based on your experience?

2. What are some unique strengths that you have observed in female leaders? How can women use these strengths more effectively to gain respect and advance their careers?

Part 3: What Not to Do

CHAPTER 12

Getting Emotional

Personal Reflection

1. On a scale of 1–10, how would you rate your emotional strength in difficult or threatening situations? What are your typical responses to stress in your personal life, in your professional life? What tips will you practice to calm yourself and develop greater emotional strength? What will success look like for you?

2. What have you observed about female responses to stress in your personal and professional life? How can you practice leadership and help family members, colleagues, and direct reports develop emotional strength?

Group Discussion

1. People often avoid sharing critical information with leaders who lack emotional control. Have you experienced or observed this? If so, describe your experience and the effect in the workplace. What strategies can leaders practice to diffuse emotion and focus on results?

2. What are the problems and pitfalls when women try too hard to please others, when leaders are afraid that others won't like them? How have you seen these attitudes affect the workplace? What was the impact on departments, teams, and the company? How can leaders be more effective in decision making in the midst of conflict?

Questions for Men

1. In your opinion, what does emotional strength look like? Why is this important? How would you rate your own emotional strength? What influences have helped you develop your emotional strength? How do you influence other men and boys in this realm?

2. How important is emotional strength for female leaders? Describe situations when women leaders have demonstrated success in crises or challenging situations. What qualities and behaviors did you observe? Describe situations when women leaders lacked emotional strength. What were the behaviors, and what was the effect in the workplace?

CHAPTER 13

Overthinking Your Decisions

Personal Reflection

1. Evaluate your tolerance for risk in decision making. Do you make decisions based on how you feel or on research and information? What tips will you use to control emotions and become more objective in making decisions?

2. Do you "waffle" when others challenge your decisions? What criteria should you use to determine when to stay the course and when to adjust your strategy or direction? What tips will you use to improve your strength and confidence in making decisions? What decisions do you need to make today?

Group Discussion

1. Discuss the 80 percent rule in decision making. Have you used this method? If so, share your experience and results. Share other guiding principles you have used in decision making.

2. What are the characteristics of a controlling leader who is afraid to make mistakes? What are the damaging effects of controlling or micromanaging? What are one or two strategies a controlling person can use to improve his or her leadership?

Questions for Men

1. Have you observed any general differences in decision making with male and female leaders? If so, what tendencies have you observed? What are some best practices you can share to improve decision making?

2. How do you respond when others criticize your decisions? What can you share about your own process of sound decision making? How and why has this been effective for you? How did you develop your process for decision making?

CHAPTER 14

Using Upspeak and Other Annoying Habits

Personal Reflection

1. Assess your communication style in the workplace. Do you use upspeak, use "like" frequently, or use feminine sounds to soften your message? Consciously listen to yourself during discussions and presentations. How will you strengthen your communications by intentionally improving the use of your voice?

2. Reflect on your use of body language—eye contact, posture, use of hand gestures, and facial expressions. Do these strengthen and support your message or detract from it? Ask a trusted coworker to provide feedback for you, or watch a video of yourself if you can. Determine where you need to improve, and be aware of this in presentations, meetings, and one-on-one discussions.

Group Discussion

1. What have you observed about voice inflection (upspeak, girl speak, etc.) in the workplace? How about the frequent use of "like" or other feminine language and topics? What effect do these habits have on communication? How do you view leaders who exhibit these habits? In contrast, what are the qualities of leaders who deliver strong and credible messages?

2. Discuss body language—eye contact, posture, use of hand gestures, facial expressions, and positioning of the head. What unconscious habits detract from a credible message? How can female leaders improve their communication, and what is the single most important action to take? What are other gestures that support a powerful and passionate message?

Questions for Men

1. What annoying voice habits have you observed in the workplace? What is the effect of these on credible communication? How can these undermine a powerful message? What suggestions can you offer to help leaders improve the use of their voice in presentations, meetings, and one-on-one conversations?

2. What differences have you observed between male and female leaders in the use of body language (eye contact, hand gestures, posture, facial expression, etc.)? How do these gestures support or detract from a credible message? What do you think are the most important things women can do to improve communication?

CHAPTER 15

The Gender Game

Personal Reflection

1. Honestly assess your strategy in dressing for the workplace. Is your foremost thought how to be noticed or how to be professional? Could your attire be perceived as sexy or frivolous? What wardrobe adjustments could you make to support your professional image?

2. Have you become distracted by playing the "blame game" in the workplace? What should you start doing to stay focused on results? What are the current obstacles for you, and how will you produce results in spite of them? How can you become a leader in results thinking among women in the workplace?

Group Discussion

1. What is the suggested attire for female professionals in your industry? What do you observe about the attire of female executives in your company and other companies? How can women apply these concepts in planning their professional wardrobe? What do you think are the big no-no's in workplace attire?

2. What strategies have you used to navigate around obstacles in the workplace? If appropriate, share how you have experienced gender bias, and what you did or could do to break through this barrier. What forward-thinking strategies can women use as opposed to blaming, complaining, and staying stuck? How can women lead and succeed despite the inevitable barriers?

Questions for Men

1. What barriers have you faced in your career development? How did you respond to these, and what strategies did you use to move forward? Have you experienced gender discrimination, and how did you respond to this? What have you learned that can help other leaders respond successfully to gender discrimination?

2. What observations and suggestions can you offer about professional dress for men and women? What are the suggestions for your company, industry, and for meetings with clients and conferences? In what ways can attire sabotage success?

Part 4: What to Do

CHAPTER 16

BE A STRATEGIC THINKER

Personal Reflection

1. Which strategic-thinking qualities are the strongest for you? How do you currently utilize these strengths in your workplace? What are some additional applications for your strengths? How can you more effectively influence outcomes using these strengths?

2. Which strategic-thinking qualities are the weakest for you? What actions could you take to improve these areas? What is the single most important step you could take? When will you start?

Group Discussion

1. Are there some strategic-thinking qualities you think are more important than others? If so, why? How have you improved your strategic thinking during your career? What has contributed to more successful outcomes?

2. Which qualities do you primarily utilize in your strategic thinking? How did you develop these abilities? Which qualities do you observe in colleagues or other team members? How does the blend of these qualities contribute to a better outcome?

Questions for Men

1. Do you think there are any discernible differences between how men and women approach strategic thinking? If so, what are the differences? How can these differences contribute to a more successful outcome for teams and companies? How might the differences create resistance?

2. What has surprised you about the unique thought process of colleagues? What have you learned from others about strategic thinking? How have you used this information to improve your strategic thinking?

CHAPTER 17

Communicate with Power

Personal Reflection

1. Is your professional language powerful or "soft"? What words can you utilize to create more impact in your communication? Evaluate the number of words you use. Do you over-explain or give too much detail?

2. Read through e-mails you've sent recently. Can your e-mails be improved? If so, edit them to remove unnecessary words and insert power words. Use what you've learned to write more effective e-mail communications.

Group Discussion

1. As a group, edit the phrases in the "Power Language" exercise on page 150. How can the phrase be more concise? What power words can add impact? Why is this important?

2. What effect can powerful communication have on career development, on leadership success? Why? Are there any cautions in using powerful language? If so, what and why?

Questions for Men

1. Do you think there are different levels of "power" words to use, depending on the situation? If so, why? Describe the situations. If not, why? Explain.

2. How have you personally learned to use power words? What have you observed about the use of power words in the workplace? What is the effect of too many words? What are the outstanding qualities of effective communication?

CHAPTER 18

Change What You Can Change

Personal Reflection

1. What are changes that would be beneficial to your company, department, and team? What changes are possible within your realm of influence? How can you be proactive for changes in your current position? Who should you work with, and what process should you follow? What specific actions can you take?

2. What unique talent, training, and skills do you possess? Where and how can you use these to drive changes that produce better results? What are you afraid of as you think about achieving these goals? What, specifically, do you hope to achieve? What will success look like? When and how will you begin?

Group Discussion

1. What are the characteristics of passive, reactive, active, and proactive leaders? How can leaders discern when to be active and when to be proactive? How do reactive leaders affect the people around them? How can leaders self-correct when they find themselves in a reactive situation?

2. Are there situations in which leaders should be passive? If not, why? If so, why? What are the dangers of driving change outside your realm of influence? How can proactive leaders assist others with change?

Questions for Men

1. How can leaders discern where to use their energy and expertise to initiate change? What are the best ways to approach change? What processes produce successful outcomes?

2. What happens when leaders tolerate dysfunction? What is the result when leaders are passive until anger or frustration motivates them? Contrast this approach with that of a proactive leader. What are the results of each? What actions can reactive leaders take to change their approach?

CHAPTER 19

Quit Being Boring: Lead with Style

Personal Reflection

1. What are some of your unique qualities? What attracts people to you? How can you use these unique attributes to distinguish yourself as a leader? At the core, what do you know about the authentic "you"? If you are true to your authentic self, what changes do you think this will create? What do you need to do more of?

2. As you lead, where is your primary focus—on yourself or on others? What are some things your team, direct reports, and company needs? How can you use this information to lead with energy and passion? What things do you need to stop doing? What do you need to start doing? What will success look like?

Group Discussion

1. What is the impact for individuals or organizations when people lead with energy, passion, and style? What are some unique and surprising characteristics of leaders you have known? How have these leaders leveraged their strengths to wow and inspire others? What did you learn from this?

2. What is the effect of boring meetings on motivation, energy, and passion? What meeting innovations have you experienced that helped you to focus, pay attention, and contribute? What additional changes can you think of to make meetings more interesting, engaging, shorter, and more productive?

Questions for Men

1. How important do you think style is to leadership? What does style mean to you? What does it look like in professional leadership? How have you discovered your own style? How have you developed it and what impact has this had?

2. How do great leaders demonstrate passion in their body language? What are the specific physical gestures and movements that show confidence? What gestures and movements show a lack of confidence? How does each of these affect teams, meetings, and leadership success? What are the most important things for leaders to improve?

CHAPTER 20

Consider a Leadership Coach

Personal Reflection

1. What are some of the most important challenges you currently face in your career development? Considering the information in this chapter, is a mentor or a coach the best choice to help you now? Does your company provide a mentor or coach? If so, how will you advocate for one? If you own a company, how will you finance a coach or a mentoring program?

2. What are your leadership and career goals for the next 3–5 years? How will a coach or mentor, or both, provide the guidance and perspective you need to create your path forward? What is getting in the way, and what resources can enhance your discovery?

CONSIDER A LEADERSHIP COACH

Group Discussion

1. Have you worked with a mentor or coach or both? What were the benefits of each? Was one approach more beneficial for you? If so, why? If you worked with a coach, was it a personal/life coach or business coach? How did you benefit from this work?

2. Have you worked with mentors in your company or outside your company, in your industry or outside your industry? Have you worked with women mentors, men, or both? Talk about the benefits of different kinds of mentors. How do you know what kind of mentor you need and when?

Questions for Men

1. How have you found the guidance necessary to advance your career? How have mentors or coaches been part of your strategic plan? How often have you worked with a formal mentor, and how often have friends or colleagues mentored you?

2. Who has helped you face the truth when you are chasing the wrong thing? Who has surprised you by becoming a valued mentor? How many mentors have you worked with in your career? Have you worked with a coach? If so, how did this benefit you?

CHAPTER 21

Know When to Change Course and Evolve

Personal Reflection

1. Assess your leadership over the past year or two. Are there any recurring problems you should analyze more deeply? If so, what is the pattern? Is the problem in your realm of influence or control? If so, what systems, communications, processes, and strategies can you develop to mitigate the problem and change future results?

2. Think about your job satisfaction in your current position, company, or industry. Why do you do what you do? What gives you the greatest fulfillment? Is this the best you can do with your gifts, talents, and interests? Is there something else you'd like to accomplish? Is there a career dream you've yet to fulfill? If you go in that direction, what is the next step you will take?

Group Discussion

1. What is the importance of a diverse network? How does this further your mission and goals? How do you develop and support your network within your company? How do you develop and support a broad and diverse network outside of your company? How do you maintain the network you've developed?

2. What is the disadvantage for professionals who neglect network development? How do you stay in sync with your company and people? What is the danger of being out of touch? What are the symptoms? What strategies help you to be aware and to listen? How do you discern shifts in culture, motivation, and people? How do you use this awareness to excite and inspire others, to support and empower teams?

Questions for Men

1. Have you experienced a hostile workplace environment? If so, what were the symptoms? What can a leader do in this situation? What are the important considerations? What supports can help to develop an action plan? What steps should be taken?

2. What are the dangers of running on autopilot? What are the effects on your teams, direct reports, and company? How do you keep your thinking fresh and innovative? How do you challenge yourself to think differently? How can you balance stability with the right amount of change and forward thinking?

www.ingramcontent.com/pod-product-compliance
Lightning Source LLC
Chambersburg PA
CBHW060402190526
45169CB00002B/707